NATIONAL GEOGRAPHIC

Feeding Time

Dominic Loughrey

It is **10 o'clock.**

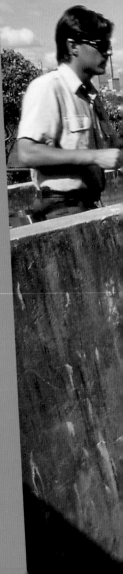

It is time to feed the seals.

3

It is **12 o'clock**.

It is time to feed the pelicans.

It is **2 o'clock**.

It is time to feed the giraffes.

7

It is **4 o'clock.**

It is time to feed the penguins.

It is **6 o'clock.**

It is time to feed me!

10 o'clock

12 o'clock

2 o'clock

4 o'clock

6 o'clock